Deeper

Thoughts

by

Jack Handey

HYPERION

New York

D0043613

Text Copyright © 1993 by Jack Handey
Illustrations Copyright © 1993 by Superstock, Inc.

10 9 8 7 6 5

Library of Congress Cataloging-in-Publication Data
Handey, Jack
   Deeper thoughts : all new, all crispy / by Jack Handey.
       p.   cm.
     ISBN 1-56282-840-1
     1. American wit and humor.   I. Title.
PN 6162.H265   1993
818´.5402—dc20   92-45721
                                        CIP

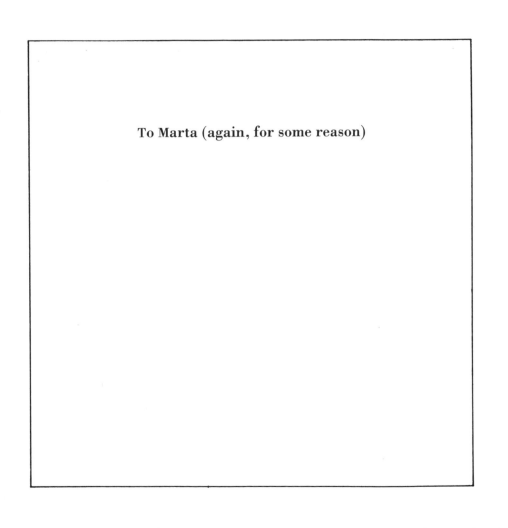

To Marta (again, for some reason)

SPECIAL THANKS to: George Meyer and Maria Semple; John Fortenberry and Melissa Christopher; Lorne Michaels; William Novak and family; Chris and Maria Hart; Christine Zander; Ian Maxtone-Graham; Lori Jo Hoekstra; Tom Gammill; Max Pross; Becky Sue Epstein; Evie Murray; Jennifer Meyer; Aaron Stielstra; Stephen Randall; Kevin Murphy; and, most especially, Marta Chavez Handey.

MAYBE in order to understand mankind, we have to look at the word itself. *Mankind.* Basically, it's made up of two separate words—"mank" and "ind." What do these words mean? It's a mystery, and that's why so is mankind.

CHILDREN need encouragement.
So if a kid gets an answer right,
tell him it was a lucky guess.
That way, he develops a good,
lucky feeling.

IF YOU ever drop your keys into a
river of molten lava, let 'em go,
because, man, they're gone.

I THINK a good novel would be where a bunch of men on a ship are looking for a whale. They look and look, but you know what? They never find him. And you know why they never find him? It doesn't say. The book leaves it up to you, the reader, to decide.

Then, at the very end, there's a page that you can lick and it tastes like Kool-Aid.

MARTA talks about sensuality, but
I don't think she'd know
sensuality if it bit her on the ass.

IT'S EASY to sit there and say
you'd like to have more money.
And I guess that's what I like
about it. It's easy. Just sitting
there, rocking back and forth,
wanting that money.

I THINK a good gift for the
President would be a chocolate
revolver. And since he's so busy,
you'd probably have to run up
to him real quick and hand it to
him.

WHETHER they ever find life there
or not, I think Jupiter should be
considered an enemy planet.

IF YOU lived in the Dark Ages, and you were a catapult operator, I bet the most common question people would ask is, "Can't you make it shoot farther?" No. I'm sorry. That's as far as it shoots.

WHY IS IT that we will laugh at a man in a clown outfit, but we won't laugh at a man just walking down the street carrying a clown outfit in one of those plastic dry-cleaner bags?

PROBABLY the earliest fly swatters
were nothing more than some
sort of striking surface attached
to the end of a long stick.

INSTEAD of trying to build newer and bigger weapons of destruction, mankind should be thinking about getting more use out of the weapons we already have.

THE CROWS seemed to be calling
his name, thought Caw.

IF YOU GO flying back through
time, and you see somebody else
flying forward into the future,
it's probably best to avoid eye
contact.

TO ME, it's a good idea to always carry two sacks of something when you walk around. That way, if anybody says, "Hey, can you give me a hand?" you can say, "Sorry, got these sacks."

WHENEVER someone asks me to define love, I usually think for a minute, then I spin around and pin the guy's arm behind his back. *Now* who's asking the questions?

I REMEMBER we were all horrified
to see Grandpa up on the roof
with his Superman cape on.
"Get down!" yelled Uncle Lou.
"Don't move!" screamed
Grandma. But Grandpa
wouldn't listen. He walked to
the edge of the roof and stuck
out his arms, like he was going
to fly. I forget what happened
after that.

IF YOU ever catch on fire, try to avoid seeing yourself in the mirror, because I bet that's what *really* throws you into a panic.

I WISH my name was Todd,
    because then I could say, "Yes,
    my name's Todd. Todd
    Blankenship." Oh, also I wish
    my last name was Blankenship.

IF YOU'RE an ant, and you're
    walking along across the top of a
    cup of pudding, you probably
    have no idea that the only thing
    between you and disaster is the
    strength of that pudding skin.

DAD ALWAYS thought laughter was
the best medicine, which I guess
was why several of us died of
tuberculosis.

I DON'T think God put me on this planet to judge others. I think he put me on this planet to gather specimens and take them back to my home planet.

JUST BECAUSE swans mate for life, I don't think it's that big of a deal. First of all, if you're a swan, you're probably not going to find a swan that looks that much better than the one you've got, so why not mate for life.

IF YOU'RE robbing a bank, and
your pants suddenly fall down, I
think it's okay to laugh, and to
let the hostages laugh too,
because come on, life is funny.

JUST AS bees will swarm about to protect their nest, so will I "swarm about" to protect my nest of chocolate eggs.

IF YOU were a gladiator in olden days, I bet the inefficiency of how the gladiator fights were organized and scheduled would just drive you up a wall.

SOMETIMES I think I'd be better off dead. No, wait. Not me, you.

SOMETHING tells me that the first mousetrap wasn't designed to catch mice at all, but to protect little cheese "gems" from burglars.

I CAN'T stand cheap people. It makes me real mad when someone says something like "Hey, when are you going to pay me that hundred dollars you owe me?" or "Do you have that fifty dollars you borrowed?" Man, quit being so cheap!

YOU CAN'T tell me that cowboys, when they're branding cattle, don't sort of "accidentally" brand each other every once in a while. It's their way of letting off stress.

ONE DAY one of my little nephews came up to me and asked me if the equator was a real line that went around the Earth, or just an imaginary one. I had to laugh. Laugh and laugh. Because I didn't know, and I thought that maybe by laughing he would forget what he asked me.

IF I COME back as an animal in my
next lifetime, I hope it's some
type of parasite, because this is
the part where I take it *easy*!

I THINK the mistake a lot of us make is thinking the state-appointed psychiatrist is our "friend."

WHEN YOU first start wearing a turban, probably the most common mistake is wrapping it too tight. You have to allow the head to breathe.

IF YOU GO through a lot of
hammers each month, I don't
think it necessarily means you're
a hard worker. It may just mean
that you have a lot to learn
about proper hammer
maintenance.

WHEN PEOPLE say that the desert is lifeless, it just makes me want to grab them by the collar and yell, "Why you stupid, stupid bastard!" Then I drive them out into the desert to where the circus is, and point out the many forms of zebra and clown life.

IF THERE was a big gardening convention, and you got up and gave a speech in favor of fast-motion gardening, I bet you would get booed right off the stage. They're just not ready.

WE LIKE to praise birds for flying. But how much of it is actually flying, and how much of it is just sort of coasting from the previous flap?

INSTEAD of raising your hand to ask a question in class, how about individual push buttons on each desk? That way, when you want to ask a question, you just push the button and it lights up a corresponding number on a tote board at the front of the class. Then all the professor has to do is check the lighted number against a master sheet of names and numbers to see who is asking the question.

IF YOU'RE a boxing referee, it's
probably illegal to wear a bow
tie that spins or changes colors.

YOU KNOW something that would really make me applaud? A guy gets stuck in quicksand, then sinks, then suddenly comes shooting out, riding on water skis! How do they do that?!

WHETHER they live in an igloo or a grass shack or a mud hut, people around the world all want the same thing: a better house!

WHEN YOU'RE going up the stairs and you take a step, kick the other leg up high behind you to keep people from following too close.

WHEN RICK told me he was having trouble with his wife, I had to laugh. Not because of what he said, but because of a joke I thought of. I told him the joke, but he didn't laugh very much. Some friend *he* is.

IF YOU ever reach total
enlightenment while you're
drinking a beer, I bet it makes
beer shoot out your nose.

LOVE IS not something that you
can put chains on and throw
into a lake. That's called
Houdini. Love is liking someone
a lot.

IF I WAS being executed by injection, I'd clean up my cell real neat. Then, when they came to get me, I'd say, "Injection? I thought you said 'inspection.'" They'd probably feel real bad, and maybe I could get out of it.

I'M NOT afraid of insects taking over the world, and you know why? It would take about a billion ants just to *aim* a gun at me, let alone fire it. And you know what I'm doing while they're aiming it at me? I just sort of slip off to the side, and then suddenly run up and kick the gun out of their hands.

I BELIEVE in making the world
   safe for our children, but not
   our children's children, because
   I don't think children should be
   having sex.

IF YOU'RE a blacksmith, probably the proudest day of your life is when you get your first anvil.

How innocent you are, little blacksmith.

WHAT AM I afraid of? I'll tell you:
a feather. That's right, a
feather. How could anyone be
afraid of a feather, you say.
That's an honest question, and
I'll try to give it an honest
answer. First of all, did I say it
was a poison feather?

WHEN YOU die, if you get a choice
   between going to regular heaven
   or pie heaven, choose pie
   heaven. It might be a trick, but
   if it's not, ummmm, boy.

OF ALL THE warning sounds that animals make, I think the one that's the least effective on me is a kind of clicking noise.

I BET A funny thing about driving
a car off a cliff is, while you're
in midair, you still hit those
brakes! Hey, better try the
emergency brake!

I WISH there was a disease where you're afraid of clouds, because I think I could cure it. First, you sit the patient down and have a long personal talk. After that, I'm not sure, but maybe you could throw some water in his face or something.

AS THE LIGHT changed from red to green to yellow and back to red again, I sat there thinking about life. Was it nothing more than a bunch of honking and yelling? Sometimes it seemed that way.

HOW COME the dove gets to be the peace symbol? How about the pillow? It has more feathers than the dove, and it doesn't have that dangerous beak.

EVEN though I was their captive, the Indians allowed me quite a bit of freedom. I could walk about freely, make my own meals, and even hurl large rocks at their heads. It was only later that I discovered they were not Indians at all, but dirty clothes hampers.

IF LIFE deals you lemons, why not go kill someone with the lemons (maybe by shoving them down his throat)?

I WISH outer-space guys would
conquer Earth and make people
their pets, because I'd like to
have one of those little basket-
beds with my name on it.

I THINK Superman and Santa
Claus are actually the same guy,
and I'll tell you why: Both fly,
both wear red, and both have a
beard.

FRANK KNEW that no man had
    ever crossed the desert on foot
    and lived to tell about it. So, he
    decided to get back in his car
    and keep driving.

IT'S TRUE that every time you hear a bell, an angel gets his wings. But what they don't tell you is, every time you hear a mousetrap snap, an angel gets set on fire.

IF I WAS a father in a waiting
room, and the nurse came out
and said, "Congratulations, it's
a girl," I think a good gag would
be to get real mad and yell, "A
girl!? You must have me mixed
up with *that* dork!" and point to
another father.

I BET what happened was, they
discovered fire and invented the
wheel on the same day. Then,
that night, they burned the
wheel.

THE WISE man can pick up a grain of sand and envision a whole universe. But the stupid man will just lay down on some seaweed and roll around until he's completely draped in it. Then he'll stand up and go, "Hey, I'm Vine Man."

I REMEMBER how, in college, I got that part-time job as a circus clown, and how the children would laugh and laugh at me. I vowed, then and there, that I would get revenge.

IF I could be a bird, I think I'd be
a penguin, because then I could
walk around on two feet with a
lot of other guys like me.

THE BIG, huge meteor headed toward the Earth. Could nothing stop it? Maybe Bob could. He was suddenly on top of the meteor—through some kind of space warp or something. "Go, Bob, go!" yelled one of the generals.

"Give me that!" said the big-guy general as he took the microphone away. "Listen, Bob," he said. "You've got to steer that meteor away from Earth."

"Yes, but how?" thought Bob. Then he got an idea. Right next to him there was a steering wheel sticking out of the meteor.

IF I COME back as a horsefly, I think my favorite thing would be to land on someone's lip. Even if they smash you, ick!, you're all over their lip!

I THINK a new, different kind
of bowling should be "carpet
bowling." It's just like regular
bowling, only the lanes are
carpet instead of wood. I don't
know why we should do this, but
my God, we've got to try
something!

ISN'T IT funny how whenever we go to a county fair or a state fair, the first thing we do is see if they have some kind of pornography booth.

A QUIZ: If I am my brother's brother, who am I? (Answer: me.)

PEOPLE laugh when I say that I think a jellyfish is one of the most beautiful things in the world. What they don't understand is, I mean a jellyfish with long, blond hair.

IF YOU want to be the popular one at a party, here's a good thing to do: Go up to some people who are talking and laughing and say, "Well, technically that's illegal." It might fit in with what somebody just said. And even if it doesn't, so what, I hate this stupid party.

TO US, it might look like just a
rag. But to the brave, embattled
men of the fort, it was more
than that. It was a flag of
surrender. And after that, it was
torn up and used for shoe-shine
rags, so the men would look nice
for the surrender.

IT'S EASY to sit and scoff at an old man's folly. But also, check out his Adam's apple!

I THINK one way police departments could make some money would be to hold a yard sale of murder weapons. Many people, for example, could probably use a cheap ice pick.

I HOPE they never find out that lightning has a lot of vitamins in it, because do you hide from it or not?

THERE ARE many stages to a man's life. In the first stage, he is young and eager, like a beaver. In the second stage, he wants to build things, like dams, and maybe chew down some trees. In the third stage, he feels trapped, and then "skinned." I'm not sure what the fourth stage is.

I WISH I would have a real tragic love affair and get so bummed out that I'd just quit my job and become a bum for a few years, because I was thinking about doing that anyway.

IF ALIENS from outer space ever come and we show them our civilization and they make fun of it, we should say we were just kidding, that this isn't really our civilization, but a gag we hoped they would like. Then we tell them to come back in twenty years to see our *real* civilization. After that, we start a crash program of coming up with an impressive new civilization. Either that, or just shoot down the aliens as they're waving good-bye.

LIKE JEWELS in a crown, the precious stones glittered in the queen's round metal hat.

I WISH I could shrink down to the
size of an ant. And maybe there
would be thousands of other
people shrunken down to ant-
size, and we would get together
and dig tunnels down into the
ground, and live there. But
don't ever call us "ants,"
because we hate that.

IF YOU'RE traveling in a time
   machine, and you're eating corn
   on the cob, I don't think it's
   going to affect things one way or
   the other. But here's the point
   I'm trying to make: Corn on the
   cob is good, isn't it.

I BET IF you were a mummy wrapper in ancient Egypt, one thing you would constantly find yourself telling people would be, "Be sure, before I start, you have all the jewelry and so forth on the body, because I am *not* unwrapping him later."

IF YOU'RE ever selling your house, and some people come by, and a big rat comes out and he's dragging the rattrap because it didn't quite kill him, just tell the people he's your pet and that's a trick you taught him.

IF I HAD the time to sit down and
   write a thank-you note to
   everyone who sent me a nice,
   expensive present, what a
   wonderful world that would be!

YOU KNOW one thing that will
really make a woman mad? Just
run up and kick her in the butt.
(P.S. This also works with men.)

IT SEEMED to me that, somehow, the blue jay was trying to communicate with me. I would see him fly into the house across the way, pick up the telephone, and dial. My phone would ring, and it would be him, but it was just this squawking and cheeping. "What?! What?!" I would yell back, but he never did speak English.

IF YOU'RE in a war, instead of throwing a hand grenade at some guys, throw one of those little baby-type pumpkins. Maybe it'll make everyone think of how crazy war is, and while they're thinking, you can throw a real grenade.

I HOPE life isn't a big joke,
because I don't get it.